Late in a Slow Time

Late in a Slow Time

Carole Glasser Langille

The **Mansfield** Press

National Library of Canada Cataloguing in Publication

Langille, Carole Glasser
     Late in a slow time / Carole Glasser Langille.

ISBN 1-894469-13-5

     I. Title.

PS8573.A557L37 2003   C811'.54   C2003-901504-1
PR9199.3.L3238L37 2003

     Text and Cover design by Tim Hanna
     Author photo by Elizabeth Mills
     Cover painting *Fenêtre ouverte sur la Seine* by Pierre Bonnard
     courtesy of Le musée des Beaux-Arts de Nice

The publication of *Late in a Slow Time* has been generously supported by
The Canada Council for the Arts and
the Ontario Arts Council.

Poems have been published in the following journals: *Canadian Literature, Malahat Review, Fiddlehead, Event, Our Times, Vintage l999 Gaspereau Review, Pottersfield Portfolio, Hubbub, European Judaism, The Café Review* (Spring 2000 — Canadian Poetry), *Neue Sirene* (poems translated into German by Dieter Plumacher). Poems have appeared in the following anthologies: *Following the Plough: Recovering the Rural* (Black Moss Press), *Landmarks: An Anthology of Atlantic Canadian Poetry of the Land* (The Acorn Press), *Words Out There: Women Poets in Atlantic Canada* (Roseway Press), *A Celebration of Women in the Arts* (Talking Marigold and Mother Tongue Books), poems performed on International Women's Day, 2001, *Waging Peace, Poetry and Political Action* (Penumbra Press), *Larger Than Life,* (Black Moss Press, 2002).

Mansfield Press Inc.
25 Mansfield Avenue
Toronto, Ontario, Canada
M6J 2A9
Publisher Denis De Klerck
www.mansfieldpress.net

Printed in Canada

For Bill

and for my sons, Caleb and Luke

To Anne,

Thank you for
being in the audience,
and for responding
so deeply.
All my best,

Carl

Late in a Slow Time

II

III

IV

V

that we are all late
in a slow time,
that we grow up many
And the single
is not easily
known.

Charles Olson
Maximus, to Himself

TOO LATE

Already it is too late
to start over. So many people
I'll never be, things I won't do.
Why list them? Soon the years ahead
will be too few to manoeuvre among
and I won't be able to lie, even to myself.
As in a cave at low tide, echoes resound,
not in the spaciousness of possibility,
but in limitation. And isn't this good?
To say, *Yes, I haven't. That's right,
I never did.*

JOAN

Odd the way she put down the bowls
and looked out the window, listening for horses.

On which path did she ride?
In a country crowded with bandits, famine,
did the voice whisper *One: Power,*
mount your horse?

It's the private moment that defines her:
how she lay on her pallet beside her men
staring into the dark,
smiling at what only she could see.

Wherever she looked
the world became breath,
its very stirring, votive.

When she entered the city
the king had already deserted her,
but sun drummed in the sky.
Long before the match was lit,
she was on fire, intimate with God.

It is possible to slide backwards and down
at the very moment you clutch a hold to go on.
Forgiveness. Surrender.
She saw the road. She knew the turn.

So when flame with its blazing reach
took her in its arms, wrapping around her,
she went. Fire could only grasp her body.

Who doesn't long to stagger in shock
by burning what can no longer contain them?

YOU WANT TO KNOW HOW
MY DAY WENT, LUKE

We're waiting to drive your friends
to theatre camp, parked by a stretch of brambles and roses,
a jumble of thistles and ferns.
I'm reading my book when you tell me, *Look up.*
You know about *journeying*, that when I lived in New York
my spirit animal was deer; how one always comes
with a message. Now, when I raise my eyes
you point to a doe staring from the thicket.
It hits me again, as if I were a drum
in the hands of an ecstatic: I live in a place
deer visit, not only in spirit.
And I have a ten-year-old son
who shows me they're here.

HAPPINESS TIMES FIVE

To eat life's brevity
the way the north wind eats winter
and grows strong. Even in cold,
when I loosen my grip
I trace something unexpected.

So God paints the room lighter and lighter,
till it's bright, the good landlord,
and lets us know, when we're stripped
of how things ought to be: happiness, too,
is a sacred practice.

Snow flies in the face of the window.
Quiet blooms untouched in snow.
When I lose my hat, I retrace my steps and there it is
two days later on a post, snow-covered, frozen,
looking almost alive. Someone's watching out for me.

Who said, *We search for what's already ours?*
When I look hard at what I have
I see huge gaping holes,
and through those holes, sky
and in that sky a deep floating fathomlessness.

Everyone I've loved has told me, one way or another:
When I was tired, I slept. When I was hungry,
I ate. I went out in snow
when I was dressed for snow.
What else should I have done?

PRIVATE THEATRE

When love meets what it cannot enter
it doesn't disappear. It breaks apart:
a train hitting a solid wall.

We feel the tremor.
In dreams, houses with verandahs balance on hills,
precariously leaning.

Day has its own symbols,
harder to interpret. We can't always see,
as we would in dream,

our bodies walking toward us
surrounded by the abundance of light
the world allows us. We can't always see,

as we're heading down slopes,
the road discerns more than we do.
It veers around marshes. The hills it traverses

are more solid than ice. See how the path
continues to carry us
to where the broken, the abandoned,

the disappointed gather. All the mother of us,
all the father, attend.
Why guess why they've called us?

Who can explain what someone dies of
or why they love the way they love?
All we can do is pay our own way. Look.

Look what transforms us.
How we turn to each other. And for me,
how I managed to get off that train.

PSYCHIC POWERS

I'm going to let you
read my mind. Go ahead. You expected to see
those petroglyphs in the cave. But not that
red mountain behind,
that blood-soaked sun through misshapen trees.
Here I am climbing in the heat of the day,
looking for what's miles above when all along
what I'm searching for
rests in the shade of the trees in my yard.

Lemon and turnip in the same field,
a rope I lower myself down
to get to an abandoned beach.
There's a town that hasn't changed
in forty years. Because
there is that which does not change, lit
by candles. Light another.
Let me introduce you
to my various disguises.

Beneath this facade
an exchange takes place,
that cannot be controlled,
between myself and the world.

If minds are mirrors
reflecting one another, starting fires
that burn away the dead grass,
then can we now glimpse

the deepest self
giving and taking,
simple as breathing?

There's the *NO TRESPASSING* sign.
Trespass. Describe what you see.

PILGRIMAGE

When we walk Iona, up hills,
through mud, marble quarry, wet
grass, Mary wears a linen dress.

We walk hours. A silence set in
tansy, heather, less moss than peat.
I've never smelled air so sweet.

By stone, Bernard waits
while his mother rests. The sacred —
in words, a smile, late

setting sun. I am more inside myself
and as far out in the world
as I've ever been. A skein of light

links us. In this ancient place
I have come to believe
faith comes from the earth,

and words
with their claiming of things.
Which word holds *storm*, which

the dove of *joy* escaping?
We're visitors at the edge of place
where trades are made.

When we stop to rest,
travel washes over us
like tenderness after touch. *That fire's the light*

our names are carved in. At dusk,
Bernard trails sun all the way up Dun'I
till it sets. It was so quiet, he said,

he could hear boats pass.
And in one boat,
men talking.

A smooth crossing. In this ancient place,
blessed, where Keats climbed:
church, stone, hills, pilgrims, sheep, priests, sun, me.

LATE TO RISE

After a poem by Don Boes

Late to rise I find my muse,
disdainful, mocking.

As I fold laundry, wash dishes,
he observes me, scornful. He's my

fire alarm, my burning house,
the window where I pause to leap.

He's the leap itself, the hard ground.
When I gossip, when I laze around

he lets me know I'm a slacker,
a faker. I'm slumming.

He's a scholar. A jittery dog.
The lover who won't commit.

You're all talk, he murmurs, summing it up.
A self-proclaimed explorer, getting lost on the walk.

But just the other morning when he came to visit
he stopped time. He gave me back what I'd lost

but what was mine. Only mine.

LOOKING

I'm still looking for my parents,
trying to find roads they got lost on, strewn
with abandoned bikes and caps. Turning on the porch light at dusk,
insistent, the way a mother might call her children back
when they've wandered to another yard.

What were they robbed of as children?
I've so little to go on.
Just my angry needy father
pounding his fists on the table.
And the blinders my mother wore
to keep from being frightened.

There's a pool of things I can't forget.
I wander back on warm days.
It's coolly seductive. Like smooth stones I roll in my hands,
I keep going over events that have passed, to feel their texture.
But why search for the memories of a man who is dead
and a woman who doesn't remember?

I could weep, knowing what little comfort they found.
My middle-aged father, resentful as a kid ignored.
My hard-working, efficient mother,
distant with her daughters,
like the eldest pretending she's a grown-up.

What will say when the looking will be over?
Sun through trees?
Will the darkening pool tell me stop looking?

AS THE DOORS WERE CLOSING

Happiness slipped in as the doors were closing,
I can hide nothing from it.
Like a train pulling out of a tunnel
and bursting into light,
much that was covered is uncovered.

When the train gets stuck on a bridge
above the shaking water, I look straight down.
It's dangerous to be thirsty.
But when I look only with my eyes
water is a mirror that tells the wrong tale.

Come to me now,
you who know that the dark
is merely a gauzy curtain.
Hurry before my face and legs and arms and chest
disappear.

PHONE SURVEY

We're doing a phone survey, asking
average people like yourself, attractive, cynical, smart, etc.,
people who cook with garlic, who, if married,
it's not the first time. People who have had
two or more jobs in the last three years.
We want to know what your preferred response is
when you hear,
if in fact you do hear,
the voices. Shall I clarify?
Voices that converse
on the great unhappiness and failure
that is yours. How often
would you swear you're not drunk, no,
but the trees are swaying. We're calling to ask
if you ever get confused and mistake
the swaying of trees for the lapping of water,
until you can't get your bearing. Is that when
the voices advise you, smooth
as a nail going in? Are there certain words that,
can I say, sneak in from behind, know all
the back entrances? Would you agree
the secret of their strength
is that they will not let you give in
to your hunger? How often
all you've said and all you've done, torn
like meat from a bone. Is that when you go out, walk
past lighted windows? Go to a movie? Have a Coke?
Or do you hang around, drift off
till the voices wake you with a jolt or slap: "Payback time."
Like a street person in front of a diner, begging for change,
who will not let you go in and get your lousy cup of coffee
though the sign on the diner flashes: OPEN ALL NIGHT.

Are the voices familiar with, say,
streets you walked as a kid,
torn signs, dead trees?
We're asking if the voices, now or in the past,
have ever told you that you have to go back
to the path by the precipice. Because that is your path.
Would you mind answering? Or am I interrupting something?
Shall I call back later? What time would be best?

II

EDVARD MUNCH

We do not think of you as a great renderer
though you were. Often you preferred
to recall the scene from memory.

What did you carry with such certainty
into the canvas? Misfortune?
You melted its gold into pigment.

A torch burns in your paintings
though we don't see its blaze, just what it lights.
And, of course, all the small signs of love —

a woman on the bed sleeping it off.
Knees up, limp arm flung out. On the table
two bottles of wine. Red at the corner of her lips

as if the life force were seeping out. The desolation
of browns and beiges and yellows
the morning after.

Like a sleepwalker you wander
so we might follow in that landscape
guided by a column of moon on water. Not drawing us out

so much as leading us in
to ourselves. How delicate the bones
between neck and shoulder. Hard how such a fierce blow

comes from something soft as water.
But strength hides
in the heaviest stones. And beneath and beyond

and among — shadow. Our shadow.
From your light. From your
disconcerting gaze.

Ten thousand years
was the time a man burned in hell,
your father said. You disagreed. *It was less,*
you said, *closer to a thousand.*

MY TIME WITH PAUL THEROUX

"The shortcut through Boston that night
was a mistake." That's how we met. I was living
in a house on top of a hill. Afraid to leave,
I kept the lights on, music going.
When I went to a party I called a car service.
Not what was straight ahead,
but what I noticed from the corner of my eye
affected me most.
You talked about fish dancing upright, towns
where emus are jealous, cows are braggarts.

"I'm rice and tarragon and the one with the money. Eat," you laughed
and your laugh was deep.
I knew I'd go where you went.

A *frisson* went through me
as you brushed past on your way to your tent.
I watched as you read letters, a sad smile on your face.
You ate tinned fish, reassembled
your boat. Later, clothes steaming in the rain,
you crawled naked into your sleeping bag.
I had been walking with my companions: envy, longing.
But the bonds that tied me to these friends
were weakening. Waves
tumbled over each other. When I looked up
there they were again, in the great ocean sky.
The lost island, dark and cool,
welcomed me. Anyone there,
thousands of miles from land, knows
he or she lives at the centre of the world.

"Water, island, fish, man, back, canoe, cry, woman."
Put these words in any order and you come up
with the same sentence: *It's hard for one person
to reach another.*

"You can go almost anywhere and do almost anything
if you are not in a hurry," someone told you
and you passed that on to me.

"My stories are part overheard, part found, part remembered, " I told you.

"Here," you said. "I bring breadfruit and fish and stories
because you asked for food."

DAMP SHORE

When a man opens?
Perhaps intimacy is the most chaste
love, nothing coming between two bodies
but tremor, tidewater inching its way
up the damp shore, leaving its wrack and its mark,
its rhythmic notation.

The isthmus that pierced dark water,
the narrows over which we travelled,
led us to shore when it was nearly dusk,
legs soaked in brine.
In the weather system of mood,
in the yielding and subsiding,
love is tidal.

What's heavy-scented and specific
lingers. This need to know
what you taste like. This appetite.
A sweetness. Even light will not be quenched
as it dazzles shifting water, then lowers itself
down and down.

THE QUIET IN VERMEER

In Vermeer's paintings,
      we look through half-opened doors
            to distant rooms, anticipating
                illumination.
It's a private room we're led to
      where a woman with lute pauses
            to look out the window. So too
                woman with pitcher, woman
with pearl necklace, an astronomer
      at his table. Each alone
            on the canvas, each drawn to the light
                moving inward.
The rooms are so quiet
      you would *not* hear a pin drop
            though you could see the light glint off that pin, ruffle
                the nap of the heavy rug, glimmer
in polished gold pitchers, the lustre of pearls,
      in glazes and glasses of plum-coloured wine.
            There are satin jackets, the pigment of yolk, red dresses
            like persimmons bursting.
When the woman is not alone,
      as the girl at her music,
            she looks directly at us: *why*
                have we come?
Whose letter? Vermeer does not explain
      but we are not left in the dark. We feel the sun,
            warm on our face,
                through painted window.
This is the only light pure enough
      to fix such stillness, a stillness that captures
            the interrupted moment,
                moment of deep reflection

when a man, a woman gaze at
    an inner world
        whose light is drawn
            from a different source.
This is what Vermeer painted
    slowly, very slowly,
        in one room in a house in Delft, where he lived
            with his wife, his eleven children, his mother-in-law,
collectors coming and going
    commissioning him,
        as he kept painting and painting
            until he died in great debt at the age of forty-three.

"FUNNY, NONE OF US HEARD THE ROAR"

Wind might as well give condolences
for our short time here.
Sun, with all its strength,
does not roil water.

You and I did not go out over our heads,
though my guess is
that's where we should have gone.
We had hopes of seeing in the dark. In the day

we slept. How much time passes
before we know what's happened?
Even this takes courage: to want to hurry
but to sit very still. We know what we know.

Let me put it another way —
why force the doors
when they stand open? When we're ready,
the right maps find their way into our hands.

Do you still live with ghosts?
I do. They enter
like a heaviness
drop by drop.

Oh love, how did we live together
for so many years in that one small room? Maybe
we were the same person,
dreaming not so much of a way out

as a way in, a place that was warm enough
and safe enough
and in which, after all that time,
we could wake.

THE AUTHOR

In Shelburne, Sackville, Middle Musquodoboit
I'm introduced as THE AUTHOR to the grade twos and threes
as I stand in front of class after class
to read that fascinating epic, *Where the Wind Sleeps.*
Sometimes the room is this messy
and there isn't any wind. Ha ha.
Like someone who stutters or has had too much to drink,
I can't remember what joke I told where.

By the time I have read to five or six classes
I'm close to screaming *Who cares where it sleeps?*
Though the children, my good-natured employers,
crammed into the library, don't seem to mind.

I like your Windy book they write in thank-you notes
with picture after picture of two boys in bed.
Do you know you are right the wind has a job! Love Danielle.
Your friend Cameron. Your new friend Meghan L.
My favourite part was when wind tore off curtains.
I liked it when they said, ' I love you, goodnight.'
This about a book all of twenty-three pages, where the big action is a breeze
whistling through gates.

Questions are carefully prepared beforehand: *Where*
(as *in the world*) *do you get your ideas?*
When did you start writing? Will you visit again?
I'd like to. If only to hear grade ones
shout important things: *I went in the woods*
with my Poppy this morning. I have a kitten. My mother's a nurse.
Good news! Though teachers ask children *Please Stick To The Topic.*

How are you? Good, bad? I like all of your book. From Nicole.
It was funny having you. Is this your only job?
Do you like your story a lot? A reasonable question.

From Mrs. Simpson's grade-two class, the comments
get more and more extreme. *Your book is very cool and nice.*
I think you are the best author.
I wouldn't be surprised if it was the best book in the world.
Did you do any other books rather than the wind book?
Come back, they shout as they're led off to recess,
wind slipping through each crack open windows will allow.

PLOUGHING THE FIELD

One more of the yoked and driven animals, we plough this field
with memory, trees inflamed,
eyes adapting to sun.

We don't know why this must be done
only how to obey. We're nearly tame,
though bewildered by what soil won't yield.

What can it give? Nothing that will heal.
No name to release us. Just stone after stone that surfaces on this plain.
And the heart's possessions. Each one hard won.

SOMEWHERE IT IS WRITTEN

Somewhere it is written
we would lie down together.

You visited first in dreams. Brief message
from the future. When I started out,

your voice a map, I had no idea
where it would take me.

Three o'clock in the morning,
I cannot find you in the house of worry.

Does it rest on something solid, with its rotten roof,
its nightmares? House sleep won't obliterate.

I don't interrupt conversations.
Though I'm here I think: *this house isn't my house.*

Did I follow the circle
down to its depth? Was I stubborn, intractable?

Somewhere it was written, I had to make every false move
to keep moving at all.

That between conversations — in fact within the words *between,
beneath, below* — we would find each other.

Luck? If you call yourself the stumbling, the lake I fell into,
grass I rested on, sun warming my skin.

DEATH IS OUR MOTHER

This life that promises,
reveals, takes away is not
our real mother, clearly. Why else
all the drudge work? We learn early
she's our stepmother, always
holding something back. It's another
she favours. We can have only one
attitude toward her: patience. In time,
we learn she masks her plans with symbols.

What we inherit we carry with us,
the knowledge that each moment
everything passes. What else
is more conducive to love? Like a calyx protecting petals,
all through this life
we feel our birth mother guiding us.
Good spirits gather: near the door,
at the table, by the bed. We pinch ourselves
to see if we're awake.

Though it's a good dream
filled with hope and yearning,
though it's a vibrant dream,
one day we'll wake. We'll wake
to eat the nourishing food. We'll wake
to take what's truly ours.
We must be young
to sleep this long.

WILD DOGS

What is envy but the self
imprisoning itself?

The elm tree, the quivering aspen
know the escape route.

Water has its own hypothesis, mouthing its way
up the dry shore, humming.

Anyone whose voice is choked,
or who's lost his voice in a storm, has heard

his cry returned through different paths,
bursting with the breakers.

I'm sick with wanting.
An undertow pulls me down

to a sea as black as a sky without stars,
or with stars you wouldn't want to wish upon.

What is envy but a wild dog jumping you?
A watchdog making sure you stay where you are.

NOT IN THE WARM EARTH

This is where we come
to find our parents.
In the fine cloth. In the neat hand. Did you
make this for me, mother? Are you
proud, father? Though I didn't
hit the ball, though I didn't
go to meetings.

I lived mostly in my dreams. Remember,
I would go into the yard, my bike
a horse. I'd race. I'd vault
fences. By the time I got home,
I'd crossed the border,
was in my late thirties, children
holding both my hands.
New lock on an old door.

This is where we find our parents,
whitewater rafting down the rapids
in the same boat we're in.
But it tips, it turns over.
I can't save them.

In the middle of the night
they wake me. They tell me I've made mistake
after mistake. They're worried.
I get up. Heat milk. Tell them
I visit often. Am still touched
by incandescent moments
of their great caring, their heroic endeavours.
I know how hard it was to live
in that house. In that life.

"But, mother, it's late. Father, you're dead, it's time
you were asleep. When you do visit
you don't have to rattle the doors.
Knock gently, I'll be listening. Tell me
why you have come. What can I give you?"

III

MOTHER, WHAT YOU HELD YOURSELF BACK FROM

That luxurious ringlet you kept in your drawer
is eighty years old now. Your mother cut it off
when you were five. How long was your dark thick hair
when you rode your horses? Did you pile it up
        to bare your neck?

Lessons, maids to iron your dresses.
How could you know then,
girl who would become my mother,
that everything would crash around you when you were sixteen,
        that for the rest of your life

you would have to make do? As if the Great Depression
were a flood that kept trickling down the long years,
carrying, on its tide, memory —
how much sweeter things could have been.

Is that why, in all your photographs,
I see melancholy in your eyes?
As if sadness were a container
holding all you might have had.

Even when you were a child, driven to school by a chauffeur,
your grade-school teacher corrected you:
No, you're not Canadian. Ask your mother
where you're from.
        A Jew was foreign. A Jew was curious.

So when your horse bolted, when your handsome companion
galloped beside you, grabbed your reins,
slowed down that horse, so legend goes,
did you notice his resemblance to a famous actor,
tall, heroic? Looks mattered so much to you.

Did you think, when he finally proposed,
you'd be rescued once and for all?
In that dark house we lived in
by the schoolyard? Kids yelling

next door and throwing their hardballs,
narrowly missing our narrow kitchen,
with its formica table, five hard chairs? Not a place
you ever felt at home. And dad? How many suppers
did he storm away from, offended?

At night, smoking your one cigarette
in the half light, reading your paper. To my exasperation,
crying. And then, in a flash,
you're old. Sitting on the couch snarling at dad,
who, you make perfectly clear, is useless to you.
"Now, I'll never amount to anything," he says,
almost ninety, hunched on the couch beside you.

My beautiful tall mother in the photograph
holds my three-year-old hand
and smiles and smiles and still looks sad.
Surely she could not have known what was to become of her,
how she would forget and forget in the Home for the Aged.

"Where is that man?" she asked,
without any warning, last time my sister came to visit.
"You mean George, your husband? He's dead," my sister says.
"Oh, he's dead," my mother says, disappointed. Then she perks up.
"We had some fun times together," she nods, musing to herself.

Eric Rohmer's SUMMER

A beautiful but dazed young woman,
lonely, bewildered, wonders —
for the entire movie — where she'll go

for her vacation. That's it. All is slow
conversation, confusion, blunders.
She cries repeatedly, spies omens

around every corner. Hard, not human
how the gods separate us, send us to plunder
oceans for roses, the desert for snow.

AVALANCHE

She came every other Friday
to clean, Roxanne, a slender, pretty woman
with skin the colour of coffee.
We'd sit in the kitchen after the floor was dry,
talk about boys in my class,
songs I liked. I watched TV, dreamed. No plans. M&M's.
Waited for my mother
to get back from work.

"You should be cleaning your room more,"
Roxanne said, looking at the heaps of clothes
piled on the floor.

After school she made pudding
measured with a teacup, portions
always too sweet. She'd be finished
vacuuming and gone
before my mother got home.

Some days she'd bring Peaches,
her boyfriend's daughter,
who would nap in my parents' room.
Once I walked into that room and rocked that child's shoulder
till she woke, surprised.
"Now why'd you go do that?" Roxanne scolded. "A grown girl,
nearly ten, waking a three-year-old?"

Why *did* I wake her? Why do I remember
that shred of conversation as if it had to be repeated
across the avalanche of years?

So many mothers I adopted along the way,
like Roxanne, who showed me
a clean and orderly world,

though it wasn't my world.

What I do now is sift the remains —
how she looked then,
the dust of her name.

FROM THE UNKNOWABLE

one is known. The breeze
spreads leaves of the ash, jostles water
along the boat's prow. On the beach, one bough lies hollow,
an open thigh
    wind blows into.

In the sky, colours of the river gather.
There is no wildness equal
to embraces we shared in the dark by the river.
With each loss of breath
    I am filled

with an extravagant breathless strength.
How we work what we love. I've just begun to notice
where we've disembarked. And there is nothing
to hold on to. Even here,
    love. Even here.

Oh world. Cold water. Hard wind.

ARIADNE

When I close my eyes I sink
into a hole so black I can't imagine
I'll ever get out. I'd ask the question
but I don't *know* the question. There's a knife in my mind
and it's slashing my wrist. NO is what I've come up against,
and the deeper I go the louder it gets
until it's an ocean of sound so enormous
the person I love is floating away
getting smaller and smaller. That tiny speck out there
is a boat that won't turn around
no matter how long I wait.

When I lie down on my bed of dreams
ghosts haunt me.
But delusion is a sly host;
I know what it's like to live in that house.

I've weighed, on a scale,
again and again: this is what he wanted,
this is what he took.
And in that space where his promises ripened,
nothing but darkness
and a hollow echo
and all my efforts, aborted, stilled.

The thread I gave him,
the thread he left behind,
is the very one that binds me to him
so tightly I can't move.

Take it, I told him
that November morning
when we stood by the walls kissing.
Take it while it's mine to give.

It can't be broken, I said, not knowing even then
how strong it was: *this law called love
that passes through one person into another.*

AFTER HOURS

Like a protagonist in a Jean Rhys novel
who lives alone

on one of those nights spent drinking,
too tired to cook,

you're waiting — it's been years —
and no one

has moved you into the house on the hill
near the ocean, surrounded by gardens,

that lovely house. We're waiters, all of us,
at *L'Hôtel Impatience.* Or patrons. The tips are poor.

Wait, Come back, Don't leave, you cry
to some phantom at the counter.

Who taught us this, the hostess wonders,
to miss what was never ours, to miss

what was never missing? She lights a cigarette.
Once we leave she'll close up.

WORK

The very wind grinds and gnashes.
What is work? "The talisman to guard against
oneself," a Mrs. Campbell writes. She's

quoted in _A Book of Quotes._ Also Lowell,
though not which Lowell: "No man is born into the world
whose work is not born with him."

I've waitressed, been assistant to
a Dean of Engineering, horrible man,
proofread, taught. I might as well

have pushed stones uphill. Done nothing.
I've done that well. _The urn_
that keeps the ash is not impatient.

I know what doesn't work:
to want too much, to try to force.
I taught my children hurt that way.

"Unless a man works he cannot find
what he is able to do." I know what I can't do.
Though I've swept and mopped a thousand times,

look at this house!
Some people know the vow of work. Take Ray.
He's seventy. Has a business

and runs a farm. Last week
I drove with him and Marge
home from a concert. Up ahead a car stalled.

"We don't know what's wrong but we'll be fine,"
the driver said. "You go on."
He did. Then he turned to Marge: "Two women alone,

we should go back."
"No," I groaned inside my head.
"Home, home, to bed, to bed."

But he did go back. That's work.
To push through task. To take the time.
To reach and find the other side.

Consider, if we are not allowed
to plead, to trade, to take
for granted, see what a good day's work is worth.

Is love work? Like Orpheus
perhaps we can't look back
or we'll lose the living, breathing thing.

I want to know what we need to live.
Mending clothes, doing dishes,
writing poems, is this work?

HELEN TALKS TO CASSANDRA

Fear goes from the famished to the famished and has a voice
like a sheet of rain descending.
I hear it like waves smacking hard against a vessel. I know now

I'll never board the ship that sails in my name,
or begin the journey I was meant for.
We have the same name, you and I.
You too have felt like a ghost

remembering what it was like
to be a person.
But the blood. I never knew anything
could bleed this much.

How can I describe it? Because I can't help but approach,
again and again, the same inevitable
situation. What he did. What I did.
The lands that burn between us.

My legs his tongue my hair his fingers. The truth is,
his body does not press against me more heavily
than the walls that circle this city,
a city I remain outside.

Keep what I've written, will you? And my jewels.
Who knows when I'll get home again.
Though I'd like to believe, as you say,
I'm not as far away as I think.

Your voice is like your brother's,
who held me so close
when he turned his head
his lips brushed my shoulder.

When I hear it I remember
a joy that stayed with me a long time
before it drained away.
People love? Perhaps. You say, if only I could hear

who calls my name
and how haunting the sound,
like a lance piercing the air.
Too clearly, I hear. I hear.

THE BOTTOM OF THE HEART

From the bottom of my heart?
The bottom is where dark
accumulates drip by drip

until its muddy waters rise and slip
into all that is bright. There's no bulwark in the depths where
uneasiness starts.

Better linger on the surface, a little apart than descend to
what's forbidden and uncharted,
a blackness one might be tempted to sip.

RETURNED

I just returned from a place —
I don't know if you've been —
where cool hills slope blue then pool
that blue into lakes.

Have you been? Lakes same colour
as your eyes. So blue, I thought
you'd just come back. There was a
yes in the clean air,

yes in the drum of evening,
echoes settling over
the small villages like frost.
The air taut with cry.

I'd left the road, the town. No
friends. Just sound for sound's sake. If
you go, you go alone. The
private road's your own.

"You've made wrong turns," the voice said.
"Hills swerve precipitously
at night." But the turn was right.
I knew the way. Blind.

The moon was full. All night
it raked stones by the shore.
Birds sang, *See ya, see ya, wouldn't
want to be ya.*

They sang, *What have you won?* And
Have you got nothing your own?
Nerves jangled in me loud
as those raucousy birds.

I kept going. *If there's no*
message for me here I'll leave,
I thought. But there will be. Some-
thing coded, precise,

revealing. There's a place I
go before I jump the plane
familiar, parachute down,
where my story

is the only story. People
stay, but not too close. In that place,
I say I'm free. That's where I
thought I saw you.

I thought we knew each other.
That your secrets
were my secrets. Was I wrong?
Your eyes moored in a cool spring.

GROWING PAINS

Growing pains my mother said
when I told her my legs hurt.
I bent over the well and saw my face floating,
staring up. I'm here and not here.

My father agrees, *growing pains*. It does.
But even at eight I wonder
why something that was meant to happen
feels as if it should not be happening. As if bones themselves

resist the future. Something hides
beneath the clear surface. There's the lapping sound
water makes as it erodes and lays waste. And a glimmer
of what can't be translated and won't reassure.

Can pain be bred out of the body?
You might as well say, as if your language were French,
your *pain* is bread rising in the marrow of you
and God, who is hungry, eats what you suffer.

Slowly, like a bucket lowered into water,
I learned feeling all alone had a taste
and the taste was cold. But hunger bound me to itself,
forced me to separate reflection from reflection,

go inside, fill the empty bowls.

SUPERMAN'S WEDDING NIGHT

Having fun yet? Man of Steel,
faster than a speeding bullet,
however you disguise yourself,
tonight you must take off your clothes.
Will that be a relief? Uncertainty —
the one tall building even you can't leap
in a single bound. Hey, don't spy on your wife
through the closed bathroom door.
And careful with the heat vision.

But you've always been careful
not to hurt anyone with your enormous
strength — that's what makes you
such a great guy! Most people aren't even aware
their power is their own. Tonight
you're nervous, but willing. But listen,
this is not a night for nervous men.
Maybe your wife's fantasies, too, involve
pretending one thing and doing another. Let's hope so.

You pretend you've been before
to this chamber of passion, chamber of secrets.
You've always been able to see through doors.
Now you can read what's written
on someone's skin, damp beneath a silk slip.
Your wife's fingers delicate, smelling of mint;
her closed eyelids flutter. *No one knows
what goes on in someone else's head,* you think.
Then — who could imagine such miracles or rescue
from a touch this gentle — you stop thinking.

FATE IS SOME HUGE MACHINE
THAT IS NEVER TURNED OFF

At the hearing I'm judge and jury wondering
where the kid went in the courtroom — the one who wants to take risks,
who knows something important's at stake,
who's gotten hold of some essential information.
My life is being cross-examined. How weak it looks,
and there's no one to defend it.

But how many can disentangle themselves
from all the things that depend upon others
saying yes?

I am sorry. I am infinitely sorry again and again.
Though there's still time, I tell myself.

Time to do *what* though?

Listen, my life says to me, asserting itself at last,
as the kid wanders back into the courtroom,
there's a naked song out there
no one can decipher but you.
It's recording right now.
It's been recording all along.

IV

GLASS DREAMING

You have to wait. It may come.
The square of red light on the floor
is dreamed by glass in the window.

In towns, or by the ocean,
silence is flexible. It gives and gives,
the way the night, deepening, relaxes

and the moon unloosens
each wave's sheer veil.
A big round voluptuous moon.

That's not a ditch we walked beside
but crescendo's mad home,
the dark a shade of aubergine, air full of chorus,

the peepers' orchestration — loud
as the purple of rotting orchids.
How fine-tuned this unanswered world is.

On plains, arroyos teach stillness as lesson.
The chert, the shale resist me.
In each dwelling,

I've passed over one gift,
wanted another. Crossed a bridge, careless, edgy,
with every step counting, *next, next.*

Even in dreams
I've scavenged for glass
and used it to scrape my way out of a lie.

Children holler. The day grows cold.
Broken glass glitters in the yard.

All these say, *I know different things than you do.*

I always want to live in a place
that reveals its voice.
That's the secret, isn't it? To wait. To listen.

MAERSK DUBAI

Say you were in Roumania and wanted to go —
anywhere
that's free. Drink beer with an American girl
in a crowded bar. Listen
to loud American music. You're with your pals
in Spain when you
sneak aboard a boat that's leaving that day. It could be
any boat. You're nineteen.

Goodness is an old relative
who comes and goes at random
but is not invited
to stay in this house of time.

Say you're the boatswain and you see
the captain force two boys
down a ladder to a makeshift raft
on the freezing water. The boys
are begging the captain
to let them stay. One lies on the deck
and kisses the captain's feet. *We cannot live the way we live,*
you think, *and have another person's life*
worth anything.
You do not speak the language
of this captain but you tell him
Do not do this. Cold as ice in that ocean
he lets you know: one more word
you go with them.

We give alms to relieve our guilt.
Who is begging
beneath the water?

Say you see your friends forced
overboard. Fear is heavy
as iron sinking. It fingers your throat.
You're hiding behind a barrel, your glasses mirrored and milky
as pearls at the bottom of the ocean.
A man walks towards you. You're shaking.
But he does not
turn you over
to the captain. He hides you
in a room where two deckhands
smuggle food. This is how you live
to testify at the trial.

Shadow is the last
refuge of light.
Then *click*, the room goes black. Then
we're all left
in darkness.

In the courtroom you learn
fines must be paid
by owners of boats caught with stowaways.
The lawyer for the captain
insists
the boatswain speak better English.

Even in the indeterminate places
we find ourselves, we know
our lives are bound up
with the life of the world.
For this reason there's a shock because
we have come to expect
and count on decency.

"I didn't kill anyone," the captain says.
"I just made sure
they got off the boat."

It was March, the sun was shining, and
someone on board said,
even though no one could see the raft any longer,
maybe the boys had a chance
if they had water with them,
if it didn't snow or storm,
if the raft didn't sink, if it could just
stay afloat
and make it the miles and miles to shore.

"UPROAR'S YOUR ONLY MUSIC"
For S. D.

I returned to the muddy river
that doubled back on itself,
brush burning on scrub grass,
open book, black pine
where I paired words in bark. I have gone back
so I could make a careful, detailed map,
watching where I walked. But to put together
what was
is to feel the tear.

Most of the time
we are in the dark. And the dark
twin of day
is in us, shadows foundering in pools,
on the ground, holed in trees.
So the dark's fiery embrace,
and time, with its muddy river,
even as we go out like candles,
spin their life inside us.

WEST OF WINNIPEG

No bird can fight wind or weather,
or, tired, resist the cool formal open spruce.
Which is why the indigo bunting,
which rarely veers west of Winnipeg,
flew two thousand miles off its flight path. So birders tell me.
And how the song of a chipping sparrow

differs from a dark-eyed junco's,
that the sora's last three notes descend.
Spied on, recorded, followed
to where it summers and winters, tracked
past clematis, calypso orchids,
no bird can keep its secrets long.

Just last summer a rose-breasted grosbeak
flew through the cottonwood. No reason
a cardinal should have been there as well.
The faithful, in rain gear with binoculars —
aren't they pulled, too, by invisible guides
like those deep magnetic lines that run through the earth?

What is it that alights and then takes flight again?
Much as we long to name and claim things,
spring is ten days behind what it once was. We don't know
if this is the last snow of late winter or the first of early fall.
Who among us doesn't land
where the wind forces us, disoriented, a bit surprised?

HOW MUCH?

for Heda Margolius Kovaly, author of *Under a Cruel Star*

Thank you for writing. For letting me know
  you pulled yourself over the fence
in the dark, your friend hurrying behind you. When you heard
  the bullet hit, saw your friend fall,
you kept going. A young man you knew
  opened his door a crack,
said no, you couldn't stay there.

Had I to return
  to my town under cover, whom
would I seek out? In my childhood, signs:
  numbers on the arm of a woman down the block.
Judy's German father recalling, "My friend stayed behind
  to get his dry cleaning. They came for him that night."
Though my parents were safe in New York, still I asked
  "Weren't you afraid?" Ever since I learned
what happened, I've rehearsed
  what might have happened.

I trace repeatedly how we're related:
  Your Polish grandmother. A vacation on the Black Sea.
What my father's family were doing there
  I don't know. They were serfs in Russia. But their paths
crossed. I'm sure. They shook hands
  wearing prayer shawls.
You've as much as told me that was me, or almost me,
  running behind you.

I picture you making your way back to Prague,
  your shaven head hidden by a kerchief.
Told to line up to the left,
  I bolt upright. In that dream
I relinquish my grandmother, glad
  it's not my mother.

Hate. The word fuels the belly's anger.
  But I did not find hate in your words.
Even when the Bolsheviks replaced the Nazis,
  when they arrested your husband. You heard
his drugged voice, his forced confession.
  Before they led him away for the last time
he spoke to you. Sixty years later you spoke to me.

Where I live now, in Nova Scotia, they say,
  "He jewed me down." No one shudders
that sea caves are called "The Ovens." Each time
  I'm grateful I'm a Jew, though how much
do I know about this religion? Heda,
  I trace where our history converges to see
if any of your strength is in me, because
  a woman like you wouldn't give so much, you wouldn't
reach over years, over continents unless
  we were connected. You wouldn't be
so determined, so honest
  unless we shared something, even if it is only
this world, not yet recovered,
  and this Faith, which for me, is mostly in name.

TO GOD DARKNESS IS THE SAME AS LIGHT
For Wendy Varner

Since your death, we have been together
constantly. Your face round and open

as when you were well. Last week,
after your funeral, you yelled in my ear, told me

not to fall asleep while I was driving. You laugh
at my fears, danger the same nothing to you

as dust in your grave.
We go back to the class

where we met. You know as much as the instructor
and help me, step by step, strip wood.

Your third child is not yet two
and you're back working full time. It's down to a science,

how you organize things.
That was eight years ago.

For as long as I can remember,
on the path to the heart that winds uphill,

that dips through quarries and gravel pits,
I would pass an abandoned house,

moss softening the stone floor,
a stray dog near the entrance, on the hearth

a family of sparrows. I walked by many times,
the shutters banging from hinges. At your death

I stepped inside.
By the time I returned, unwashed, my clothes

smelling of moss and earth, there were new lines
on my hands, my face. From far off, an étude. When you died

I thought, *You did everything so well,*
we can only catch up to you.

RESOURCES

"And here, we are free for a while"
Derek Walcott

I'm driving to Halifax, the dark
    swathing darker trees,
pushing against a silhouette of pine, night letting it be known
    emptiness is not empty. In the sky
a festival of cloud and smoke. And a pale pink,
    reflected from lights in the city.
On the radio, news from Angola —
    seven people murdered in a diamond mine.
Even as I'm here, driving toward this tranquil city,
    a bridge tenuously forms and I'm in the other land as well,
the earth dark and stunning and packed with diamonds.
    Death as visible as this row of trees.

I'm moving *toward* someplace
    though dark has its own destination,
night itself a marriage of yearning and foreboding,
    yearning — a child bride, always disappointed.
And as familiar as I am with this highway,
    the rutted, the commonplace 103,
as so often happens I realize I'm lost,
    not because I don't know where I am —
though night makes things
    seem closer than they are —
but because there is something hard and glittering
    and crushed within me I can't reach.

It's that something that makes believers
    want to marry their Gods.
To attend. To bear witness. To hear God speak
    in the swiftness of what's passing.
But God speaks to the world slowly,
    a world not quite right in its head. A world where

what seems peripheral
  turns out to be the heart of the matter.
Where hope, poetry — that closeness between things
  till they are no longer separate —
these beckon beyond us. As on a sunny day,
  when the slickness of macadam
shimmers just up ahead.

IF YOU BELIEVE

If you believe there are certain things
one human being will not do to another
or that, once done, no one could deny them,
go to Terezin. Go to Bergen-Belsen.

Because you were told to line up on the left, in a minute
your wife, children, parents, disappear. If you don't believe
one person can die again and again. Or that, once dead, that's it, you're dead,
take a walk in Terezin. Take a walk in Bergen-Belsen.

Grown men weighing eighty pounds. Children
thrown like logs on the fire. Look what goes up in smoke.
If you think it's bad taste to speak of these things,
breathe the air of Terezin. Breathe the air of Bergen-Belsen.

Because they took you from your home in the middle of the night.
Thousands of shoes piled and sorted. The shorn hair
used to stuff mattresses. Can anyone say: *I live in a civilized country?*
See the sights at Terezin. Sightsee at Bergen-Belsen.

How the world changes. How it
goes on and on. It never happened.
It could never happen again. It could never happen here.
Spend the night in Terezin. Spend the night in Bergen-Belsen.

HOUSE, DOOR OPEN

There — on a remote hill
surrounded by land — a house, door open.
To enter, walk past fog,
through funerals, into the body.

I've wandered room to room. In one, my mother, all regret
and old clothes. No teeth. A hospital bed.
But her eyes, young,
fill with worry. Unmoving, she's all hurry.

She tells me keep walking and I will turn a corner.
Mother, I've had bad news. No more poems wrapped in letters.
Bill, whose gifts I still receive, though he sent them years ago,
has left with no return address.

And Dick — where can I find him,
now he's dead, except in this house?
But there will be no more quirky conversations.
Where does love go when it leaves the earth?

"In this house," my dead father tells me,
"you must lower your voice to a whisper
so you can feel the power of silence responding."
A silence in all its fullness reminding you:

it is absence that shares this drafty house with you,
chilled as rain on glass;
absence that asks you — give deeply, give all
because the clamourous world

will first seize, then cease.

V

WE ARE SITTING AROUND A TABLE

outdoors at a restaurant, two women, three men,
instructors at a workshop. Thrown together every day
for a week, we eat meals, go out for drinks: summer writing
camp for adults. We gossip about students, how gorgeous
this one is, how talented, who likes whom.
David says, "I hate young men; there are far too many of them."
Paul says, "I miss my piano more than my ex-wife."
From our table we watch boys swim in the pool. It's hot.
The St. John River, all silvered and flushed, makes us feel
we are as essential to this moment as the river.
Pam suggests a game. "Describe my husband," she says,
"what he looks like, where he works." We're silent.
Then Paul says, "We get to ask questions."
"Two questions," Pam says. "I answer one."

"Is everything okay?" the waitress asks.
Paul smiles. He likes Pam, with her short dark hair,
and when the waitress leaves he asks, "How many hours
after you met did you sleep with him?"
The outdoor lights, the chips and nachos,
the glasses of wine diminish and are replenished. Eventually we learn
Pam's husband is older than her father.
Suddenly we're going around the table
telling how we met our spouses. The ground shifts. The men
are making their confessions.
No one is still married to the first woman he married.
The summer evening, this sudden intimacy, the sky
that turns from orange to rose to plum
bear witness. Paul says. . . but why tell what he says?
Honesty, like every nakedness, quickens us.

"Nothing leaves the table," Paul says. Except,
in a few hours each of us will leave
and what will remain will be the news, *We're alive.*
But it's good news, it's big news, however fleeting —
we know this, even as the evening
is clothing us once more in its dark.

H-E-A-R-T

Look at its centre — all reception.
For what is it listening?
This is a package of a word
densely crammed and about to burst.
Can you see the heat rising
in steam off roads?
No, there are no roads on this plain
at the top of the hill.
Perhaps a parish nearby or farm
will shelter you.
Won't it perish, knocking so wildly,
exposed like this?
It's an art to keep beating
day in, day out, alone as it is.
Who will talk loud enough
for it to hear?
Who will find you on this hill with no road?

A HIKE IN AUTUMN

We simply wanted to go up
and come down that hill. Part geography,
part philosophy — the leaving and returning.

Three poplars, shoulder to shoulder in a field,
remained in my rear-view mirror
and a slip of the ocean, till I mounted a hill

and turned where it curved. Behind me, the warmth of sun.
Aren't memories a summit from which we can see?
The day was gold. The sky was exultant and the light,

bright orange through trees, said, *"You're rich."*
On the path, a conversation with a friend.
The collision of old ideas

and my seeing something new
simply by turning. But why tears?
Such little monumental changes:

what's scrawled in the pine-covered soil,
the gold leaf, the sun
trapped behind trees in a mirror. The Morse code

of one hundred and eight thousand times
the heart beats in a day. When I came home
I opened the paper. I was looking for work.

It's silly to calculate
security, to pretend we're unprotected. To resist
being on the verge of giving way.

Though I wander in places
where strength is hidden, where it's dark
and I get lost.

Help me, I whisper.
I do, God says. *Every day.*
See how I help you cry.

RIMBAUD

We meet again, Arthur, on this sweltering night in Paris,
your blue eyes scornful. I watch as a young man
buys you a drink. You grind out your cigarette,
neither accept nor decline.
Are you unwell? When did you last

eat? You want nothing to do with anyone
tonight, hunched over a book, frowning.
Who isn't in love with you? *The whole of literary Paris*
despises me, you scowl. *The most likely thing*, you whisper,

is that one will go where one doesn't in the least
want to go, and live and die quite differently
from what one would have wished.

For you that meant returning to Charleville
again and again as if it hid something
you'd forgotten. Mostly you found your mother,
perpetually disgusted.

What you did discover, you left for others
and headed out, almost immediately,
on an unseaworthy ship. You let your world
grow dark around you. But your poems

were lit
by lightning. Did you think they wouldn't take you
where you wanted to arrive?
They've led me

to your room, heart pounding. I knock
on your door, planning to offer my wallet,
something to eat. But when I see your mouth,
that hint of a smile, I can say nothing. I know this:

I go where the light is good, which is why
I'm here, in this bright place, where again and again
you reach me. How close you are.

In half as many years as you've been dead, I'll be dead.
Then I'll know or I won't know
the source of poetry's deep replenishment
and this love will no longer be
small as this page.

CALEB AT TEN

Savvy trader of candies, but so tender-hearted.
I get angry when you won't clean your room. All of a sudden
you blurt out: "I live to serve my Queen.
My ambitions and hopes are *nothing*
to her well-being. Our job
is to keep her well fed and rested."

When I promise to take you and Luke to a restaurant
you're so slow to get ready,
I grumble, "Let's forget dinner."
"How dare you imply I forget dinner! Dinner
is a dear friend of mine," you tell me.

Last night *you* made dinner: tuna noodle,
lettuce on the plate, a carrot. We ate
by candlelight — your suggestion.
You've been in such a good mood lately
with your one best friend,
too shy to invite anyone else over.

"You really like Greek myths that much?"
I ask when you want us to quiz each other every night.
"No," you tell me. "I like lying with you."
But then the tears, unexpected.
You don't know why you're crying, what you're afraid of.

Young boy who worries, may you read this poem at fifty.
May your smile be as fine then
as it is now when you come into my room dancing,
shirt off, skinny hips moving to a song in your head,
singing, *If I had a million dollars*

   I would buy you a green dress.

REFUSING TO EXPLAIN

I live on faith. Tonight
the ground ices. I don't slip. I wait
for night to redeem itself.
Walking in this terrain, I watch
where birds rest, the foot stops.

Sometimes the journey is so slow
it's hard to know I'm moving at all.
Schemes are honed on some invisible
lathe. And seeping into me,
like rain into night's dark heap,
this need to feel safe.

I'm good at walking so far,
I let go of what I didn't know
I was holding back. Still,
when night is treacherous,
every disappointment is an icy crevice.
That's when I pause.

Faith is an old woman
who refuses to explain herself.
She says: *What starts where you are as snow*
ends in me as rain.
She says: *Take what I give, it's yours.*

I'm dressed for this weather.
If it's as simple
as holding out my hand
in this dense and glittering place —
here. It's open.

THE MEETING

Years go by and still
we have not spoken or reconciled
our differences. I have not forgiven
much, or asked what it was
that tormented you. How at odds we were.
Brief moments coexisting, like sun
colliding with branches. We nodded;
we accommodated each other. But I shuddered
as the sun set. We were dark leaves
rustling in a cool breeze.
I'm cold. And though you're ill, I ignore
your request for coffee, tell you to get it
yourself as I rush through my chores,
eager to head out the doorway.
You're baffled. Only a short time ago
you were that handsome man in the photo
gazing at a woman outside the photo, your life
continuing like a road ahead.
You never saw — who does? — this chair, this
soiled room, this non-existent coffee.

So old, it's extraordinary. Not even old. Dead.
It's been years since you lay in that hospital bed,
toothless, your long stubbled face
a paste of regret, skin papery thin,
and asked why I am crying.
It's been years since they shovelled your ashes
into a metal box. And still
I will not look you in the face,
ask what you were hoping
when you became my father, tell you,
as your daughter, for what I keep longing.

SONG

When the river pulls itself
over rocks, through narrow creeks,
gravel in its mouth, what enters is
nothing
but light's buoyant shimmer.
It's the end of summer.

Wind twines trees, partnering them
as they creak.
Beneath heavy branches
shadows gather and seep into
nothing
but quiet's deep pools.

Twice last night I heard my name called
and once this morning
clear as a chime: *Carole.*
As long as I want
I can hold this jangle
of morning and birdsong, close
as a body. As long as I want.

I am mourning nothing
but the stillness
I haven't sat down with

and the long time the creek
inside me takes to fill

and the death of not giving
free passage: between branches —
I am that space
light passes through.

WHEN YOU'RE NOT HERE AND WHEN YOU ARE

Waking early, alone,
I crave the ripening hay in your field,
the smell of weeds tangled in brine, and along
the inland road, honeysuckle, sharp as juice
sucked from raw crabs by the cove.

Oh, the fine wet inside of your flowers
in your field after rain. The acrostic
of sifting earth with moist fingers, separating
essence from essence, a pebble
rolling in soil. I could lie around all day

wanting the brush of your lips. Between your lips,
the dark field meets a night sky. I am inside
each ragged breath and the pause between. Your legs —
a bridge to the twilight where, overhead,
stars pulse. On such cold nights

you take me as if I were spice in your coffee,
stir me, your beautiful strong arms,
your unbearable aching. I rely on the warmth of your voice
to illuminate the dark. Like a forest
that parts and cinches a road.

A clasp undone. The cat purrs.
A rustling as the leaves stir.
In the yielding light,
a pale sky warms. There.
The grassy rise is splashed with rain.

HOME

I like returning.
Though something far ahead
pulls me. You know the joke:
If you don't know where you're going,
any road will get you there.
Once my ex-husband said: "If you're lost
you haven't gone far enough."
Now, I rarely turn back.

Though once, confusing directions,
I went through a wood and came upon
what I thought was a field billowed with drifts.
Later I learned I'd walked across
the back harbour, frozen, covered with snow.
The unknown is always
drawing me closer. Always
it has held my weight, has never

let go beneath me.
On clear days I'm aware what lies beyond
accumulates, grain by grain, in what's here.
I've been given trust because,
no matter what I do with it,
I believe it's the key to this house
I was meant to live in,
a house from which I can travel.

LET ME DESCRIBE IT

Let me describe it. Don't glance back
  at the farmhouse. Uphill,
a decrepit fence, cows, some goats,
  horses. Then nothing but scrub
till the road curves. Turn right.
  What is it about this stretch of woods
that's so otherworldly? In ten minutes
  you can traverse the length. But once inside
sun from a barely visible sky
  dazzles moss, that plush, velvety cushion
so dense it seems
  not just to carpet but to roof us
with its light. Spruce and pine, uprooted,
  sprawl over paths.
Something wild lives here, and when I wander,
  even briefly,
I feel a slight unease. Will a tree fall,
  some animal lunge?
Still, I hate to leave. But how stay?
  This need to be private, unaccompanied,
but to reveal as well. Not to keep secrets. Perhaps because of,
  not despite, the solitary.
Returning to town I walk by the ocean,
  past seaweed left on shore: a tart acidy green,
almost too pungent to look at.

Notes

"Pilgrimage": "That fire's the light our names are carved in" is a line from "Apologia Pro Vita Sua" in *Black Zodiac*, by Charles Wright. "My Time With Paul Theroux": "The shortcut through Boston that night was a mistake," is from "My Other Life," by Paul Theroux. The title "Funny None of Us Heard the Roar" is a line from a John Ashbery poem. The line " How did we live together for so many years in one small room," from "Imagining Robert" by Jay Neugeboren. "Maersk Dubai": In March 1996, two Roumanian stowaways, and later a third, were forced overboard from the cargo ship *Maersk Dubai* by its Taiwanese captain. Filipino sailors hid a fourth stowaway and, when they docked in Halifax, reported the murders. The Canadian court decided it had no jurisdiction and no action was taken against the captain. The Filipinos, who were separated from their families and whose lives in the Philippines were threatened, were finally granted refugee status. The title "Uproar's Your Only Music" is a quote from Keats. "Resources": "What seems peripheral turns out to be the heart of the matter" is a quote from Marcel Proust. "If You Believe": Images are from notes by survivors in *Blood To Remember*, edited by Charles Fishman, and *Survival in Auschwitz* by Primo Levi. "Rimbaud: Lines in Italics are from Rimbaud's letters.

Acknowledgments

My deepest thanks to Brigit Kelly, for comments regarding poems, for advice to shake up the order, for great generosity, for celebrating with me. To Alexandra Thurman, James Warner, Anne Compton, Matilka Krow, Kathy Mac, Alison Smith, Eleonore Schonmaier for comments, support, inspiration. To Don McKay, for encouragement and kindness upon reading an earlier manuscript and to the generous Dennis Lee, for once again making things happen. To Marlene Cookshaw, my remarkable editor. To Denis De Klerck, my publisher who welcomed me so graciously. My gratitude to the Canada Council and the Nova Scotia Council for the Arts for their financial support while I was working on these poems.

Late in a Slow Time is Carole Glasser Langille's third book of poetry. Her last book, *In Cannon Cave* was nominated for the Governor General's Award and the Atlantic Poetry Prize. She lives in Black Point, Nova Scotia with her family.